The 7 Steps to Living Your Dream Life

Why the dreamer lives
their dream life
and everyone else gives up

Rose Light

ISBN: 979-8-9895447-1-4

First Edition: 2023

Download Your Gift Now

Discover Simple Ways to

DOUBLE Your Abundance Mindset in

1/2 the Time Without Confusion!

As a way of saying "thank you" for your purchase, I'm going to share with you a **Gift** that is exclusive to readers of The 7 Steps to Living Your Dream Life. It will help you double your 7 Steps to Living Your Dream Life mindset without confusion.

https://hello-rose-light.systeme.io/free-gift-f447d39b

*This book is dedicated to
all dreamers everywhere,
a child of the creator
of the universe.*

Table of Contents

Introduction

"Life is about discovering ourselves and enjoying each moment with gratitude. So, let's embark on this extraordinary journey to paint the masterpiece of our dream life, one brushstroke at a time."

Life is a unique and unpredictable journey. We're all busy bees buzzing through our daily routines, attempting to balance work, family, social commitments, personal interests, and, dare I say it, a little bit of 'me-time.' Especially true for those who are the superheroes in disguise - the women of the world, juggling multiple roles and responsibilities, seeking to fulfill their ambitions while nurturing those around them.

It's easy to lose sight of what truly matters in the flurry of life's hustle and bustle. To neglect the yearnings of your heart and the dreams that kindle your spirit. That's why we're here, you and I, at the beginning of an adventure - a journey into the depths of self-discovery and the heights of personal fulfillment.

It's time to dust off those dreams tucked away in the corners of your heart. Those ambitions got shelved amidst the responsibilities and tasks of day-to-day life. It's time to bring them into the light and breathe life into them. It's time to take "The 7 Steps to Living Your Dream Life."

Don't be intimidated by the grandeur of the title. This isn't some secret recipe or a one-size-fits-all solution. It's about recognizing and harnessing the power that already resides within you - the ability to sculpt the life you desire. It's about turning the dreams of 'what could be' into the reality of 'what is.'

Seven key milestones will mark our journey, signifying a transformative step toward your dream life. These instructions are not prescriptive to be rigidly followed but insights and inspirations drawn from the experiences of a diverse range of individuals, just like you and me, who dared and pursued their dreams.

These seven steps encompass a profound journey of self-awareness, self-compassion, visualization, consistent action, relationship-building, recognizing the opportunities, and the power of thoughts - emotions, actions, and life. They're a comprehensive blueprint for personal transformation, drawing upon people's real-world experiences across various age groups, cultures, and lifestyles.

As we embark on this journey, it's essential to remember that there's no rush. Personal growth isn't a race or a competition. It's a voyage of discovery to be savored and cherished at your own pace. There's no such thing as a 'quick fix' regarding personal growth. But we can build the life we desire with perseverance, patience, and positivity.

Remember that you are the artist of your life's canvas, no matter how busy your life or schedule is. The paintbrush is in your hands. It's time to create your masterpiece - one stroke at a time, one step at a time. Let's embark on this exciting journey together and embrace the power within us to live our dream lives!

Chapter 1

Getting to Know the Most Important Person in the World; "You"

"In the whispers of your soul, you will find yourself. The journey to self-discovery is where your true power lies, waiting to be unveiled as intricate as a labyrinth."

Embark on this transformative odyssey as we navigate Chapter 1 Getting to Know the Most Important Person in the World; "You." Picture it as a reflective sojourn into the caverns of your soul, where self-awareness grows like a luminous, guiding star. Here, we don't just seek to answer 'Who am I?' but delve deeper to understand 'Who could I truly be?' Together, we'll tread through vivid narratives of everyday life, gradually unraveling the intricacies of your being. So, step softly and listen to the echoes within; this is the genesis of your journey toward the life you've always dreamed of.

Unraveling the Concept of Self-Awareness and Why It's the Foundation of Personal Growth

The first step on any adventure isn't a physical move; it's a mental one. As we begin our odyssey to living our dream life, our initial stride is a voyage inward: a journey of self-discovery. Think of yourself as an explorer charting a course through the unexplored terrain of your soul.

The underpinning of this process is the concept of self- awareness. Picture an architect about to build a skyscraper. Before any construction happens, they need a blueprint, a plan detailing every floor, every room, and every window. Similarly, before building our dream lives, we need to understand the structure of our inner selves. Our values, dreams, strengths, and weaknesses are the foundations upon which we'll build our future.

Unraveling the concept of self-awareness is a critical first step. It's the process of shining a torch in the dark corners of our hearts and minds, illuminating the aspects of our personalities, emotions, strengths, and growth areas that we've often left unnoticed. Think of it as turning up the brightness in a dimly lit room; you start seeing things you never knew existed. Self-awareness does precisely that-it clarifies the spectrum of who we are, enabling us to understand what truly drives us.

Self-awareness is not just a fad or a catchphrase used in self-help books; it's the bedrock of personal growth. This critical insight into our internal working serves as a compass, helping us navigate the path to our dreams. When self-aware, we recognize what makes us happy, what energizes us, and what drains us. It helps us make informed choices that align with our authentic selves, steering us closer to our desired lives.

Meet Jessica, a high-performing executive. She worked long hours, fueled by the belief that professional success was her true calling. However, despite her achievements, she felt an unshakeable sense of emptiness. Only when she took the time to delve into self-exploration did she realize that her passion lay in creative writing. By embracing self-awareness, she realigned her life with her true desires, trading corporate boardrooms for cozy writer retreats. Today, she lives a fulfilling life, owning her dream of being a successful author.

Understanding oneself is only sometimes comfortable - confronting our fears, acknowledging our mistakes, and accepting our flaws. But as we've seen with Jessica, it's a powerful tool for personal transformation. Imagine this journey of self-discovery as an archaeological dig. It's about sifting through the layers of conditioning, societal expectations, and self-doubt to uncover the real treasure-our authentic selves. Once we discover who we are, we'll be better positioned to map out the path to our dream life. And this exploration starts here, in this chapter. Let's venture into this fascinating world of self-awareness and self-discovery, then begin our journey towards living our dream life.

The Role of Introspection, Writing in Your Notebook, and Mindfulness in Facilitating Self-Understanding

Introspection, writing in your notebook, and mindfulness are intimate companions on your journey to self-understanding.

Let's begin with introspection, the art of interrogating your thoughts and emotions as if you were a detective and your mind the intriguing mystery. It's about observing your feelings and questioning them. Let's dive deeper with an example.

Example: Alisha, our attorney, always felt her emotions bubbling under her calm exterior but never understood why. She sets aside a quiet hour for each evening after the hustle and bustle of her cases and clients. She creates a warm, inviting nook in her home office with her chair, a cozy throw, and a soft lamp. Sitting there, she asks herself: "Why did that argument in court today agitate me?" or "Why did I feel a surge of joy when I saw that old couple at the park?" At first, she struggles to find answers, but she is patient. She sits with her feelings, even when they feel uncomfortable, and eventually, insights begin to form.

Steps for Introspection

1. **Create Your Space:** Choose a time and a quiet place where you can be alone with your thoughts. Make it a routine so your mind starts to anticipate this reflective time.

2. **Ask Reflective Questions:** Dig into your emotions, reactions, and thoughts by asking yourself questions:

"What do I like, and what don't I like?"

"When am I happy?"

I'm happy when I'm thinking about...

I'm happy when I'm doing...

"What am I good at, and what am I not good at?"

3. **Be Patient and Open:** Don't rush for answers. Allow yourself to sit with uncomfortable feelings. They often hold the most profound insights.

Now, visualize your notebook as an empty vessel, waiting to be filled with your thoughts, emotions, and experiences. Your words weave together the narrative of your life with each sentence a thread contributing to the tapestry. Writing down in the notebook, especially after introspective sessions, puts the spotlight on recurring patterns. Suddenly, you might find an uncanny link between your morning mood and the quality of your day or notice a consistent drain of energy after associating with certain people.

Example: Bailey, a nurse, operates in a relentless, high stress environment. She usually shoves her emotions aside, but they become a burden over time. One day, she starts writing in her beautiful 'favorite' notebook. She writes her true feelings, thoughts, wishes, and desires daily in her unfiltered and unedited mind. 'How does she feel?' 'What does she want?' 'What are her thoughts?' Writing down on the paper helped her see herself from someone else's perspective and encouraged her to search for 'What kind of lifestyle and workstyle make her truly happy.' This is not forcing her to do things or disappoint herself, but helping her to understand who she is, then start to let her think about what she can do to make herself happy. It is okay if she cannot write every day, or she can write only on a short note. As she continues this practice, she begins to notice patterns in her responses, which leads to a deeper understanding of herself and gives her the answer to 'what she wants to do.'

Steps for You to Write it Down in Your Notebook

1. **Find Your 'Favorite' Notebook:** Choose something you look forward to writing. Make it a special place for your thoughts and feelings.

2. **Write Regularly:** Try consistency rather than length. Even just a few lines daily can provide powerful insights. Write down in your 'favorite' notebook about your thoughts, feelings, wishes, and desires to see things from someone else's view to make it easy to find out what will make you happy, like a cup of tea or a short walk in the morning, or

reading a book; then find out 'What kind of lifestyle and workstyle makes you happy.

3. **Make it a Judgement-Free Zone:** Write whatever comes to your mind without worrying about without sounding 'right' or 'smart.' This is the place to discover yourself.

Mindfulness is the gentle thread that weaves introspection and writing in your notebook together. It's being present at the moment, noticing the textures of your emotions, and suspending judgment. As you sit in a meeting, your mind buzzing with anticipation for the upcoming presentation, mindfulness invites you to feel the buzz, acknowledge it, and let it exist without attempting to suppress or control it.

Example: Clara, our single mom and teacher, often feels overwhelmed. Balancing her kids' needs and her demanding job leaves her with little time to breathe. One day, she decides to start her mornings differently: with mindfulness. As she enjoys her cup of tea, she concentrates on her breath, the warmth of the cup in her hand, and the early morning sounds around her. When her thoughts wander to the day's tasks, she gently brings them back to the present moment. These few moments of serenity set a positive tone for her day.

Steps for Mindfulness

1. **Begin With Your Breath:** Pay attention to your breathing - the inhale, the exhale, and the pause in between. This brings you into the present moment.

2. **Engage Your Senses:** Notice the smells, sounds, tastes, textures, and colors around you. Mindfulness is all about engaging deeply with the present.

3. **Practice Acceptance:** Don't judge your thoughts or try to avoid them. Observe them as they come and go and accept them without labeling them as 'good' or 'bad.'

In the chaotic orchestra of life, introspection, and mindfulness, writing in your "favorite" notebook are our personal conductors. They help us tune into our feelings, strengths, and vulnerabilities, and create harmony amidst the noise. So, let's wield these toots with intention, patience, and kindness as we carve our path to our dream life.

The Power of Your Notebook: Using Reflective Writing to Gain Insights into Your Feelings, Desires, and Thoughts

Our characters continue their journeys, their personal notebooks becoming indispensable in their voyage towards self-discovery to live their dream lives.

For Alisha, the attorney, her notebook became a sanctuary, a space to continue her introspective sessions on paper. She used the pages to record the questions she had asked herself and the answers she had discovered. This helped her see how her thoughts and life evolved over time. Her notes were sometimes short; sometimes, they were scribbled thoughts or questions, each contributing to her understanding of herself.

Bailey, the nurse, discovered the therapeutic power of writing in her notebook. When emotions threatened to overwhelm her after an incredibly challenging shift, she'd pour everything into the pages of her notebook. It wasn't always pretty, and sometimes it was downright raw. But it was honest and authentic, a true reflection of her feelings. As she read through her notes, patterns started to emerge, giving her a new perspective on her reactions and behavior.

As for Clara, the single mother and teacher, she used her notebook for mindfulness. She would start each day writing about the simple sensory details from her mindful morning tea routine: the warmth of the cup, the aroma of the tea, and the chirping of birds outside her window. The act of writing these details anchored her in the present moment and cultivated an appreciation for the simple joys in life.

These notebooks became a mirror for them, reflecting their authentic selves. The act of writing was a powerful catalyst for self-understanding. It became a visual representation of their internal worlds, providing clarity to emotions, highlighting patterns in thoughts and behaviors, and journey and a step forward toward living their dream life.

These practices are not exclusive to Alisha, Bailey, and Clara. No matter how busy life gets, we can all find hope and a bright future in the quiet corners of a notebook's pages. The power lies in the act itself: reflecting, writing, understanding, and growing. So, grab your 'favorite' notebook and let your journey of self-discovery begin.

In this enlightening chapter, we journeyed together into the realms of self-discovery, exploring introspection and truth and understanding within ourselves, tucked away within the intimate lines of our personal notebooks. Here, in solitude, we lay the foundations for our dream lives. As we turn the page, let's carry these insights and start building our lives, one thoughtful entry, one mindful moment at a time.

As we close this chapter, remember the journey to self-discovery is the first step toward living your dream life.

"Keep on asking, keep on seeking, keep on knocking, then you will be given, you will find, and the door will be opened."

-Matthew

Chapter 2

Stop Being So Hard on Yourself; Be Kind to Yourself

"Stop being so hard on yourself, be kind because you are your future self."

- Rose Light

Welcome to Chapter 2: Stop Being So Hard on Yourself, Be Kind to Yourself. This chapter unfurls a vital concept often overlooked in our quest for success - Self-Compassion. Here, we delve deep into the struggle between our inner critic and our potential ally of kindness. We'll embark on a journey, exploring the transformational power of self-kindness and understanding why it's critical in painting the canvas of our dream life. It's time to put on the gloves and start cultivating our internal garden of self-compassion. As we traverse this path, remember the journey is as important as the destination. So, let's dive in and discover how to be our best friend on this journey to living the life of our dreams.

Examining the Effects of Self-Criticism and the Transformative Power of Self-Kindness

Have you ever sat in a silent room only to hear the incessant chatter of your mind critiquing every aspect of your life? If so, you're not alone. Many of us find our harshest critic lives within us, echoing words of self-doubt and judgment that can inhibit the pursuit of our dream life.

Imagine Susan, a successful lawyer and a single mother of two. She juggles her career, family, aspirations, and an omnipresent inner critic. When a case doesn't go her way, the critic whispers, "You could've done more." When her children's grades drop, the voice murmurs, "You're failing as a mother." Every step Susan takes toward her dream life seems fraught with judgment and criticism. The same might be true for you.

But there's a way out of this self-inflicted harshness: self-kindness. A transformative power that can convert the daunting road to your dream life into a journey of empathy and understanding. Instead of reprimanding herself for the case she lost, Susan could tell herself, "You did your best with the information and time you had." Rather than feeling like a failing mother, she could affirm, "Children face challenges, too. It's a part of growing up."

The power of self-kindness is that it transforms the lens through which we view ourselves and our circumstances. It reframes obstacles as opportunities and failures as learning experiences, and criticism as avenues for growth. It allows us to meet ourselves where we are, acknowledging our efforts rather than criticizing our shortcomings.

Nurturing this transformative power isn't about turning a blind eye to our faults but understanding that mistakes are a natural part of the human experience.

They are stepping stones, not stumbling blocks, on our path toward living our dream life.

So, whether you're at the start of your journey or feel like you're losing your way amidst life's chaos, remember to offer yourself the kindness you'd extend to a dear friend. Because, at the end of the day, the road to living your dream life becomes smoother when walked with self-compassion. Stay tuned, as the next section will provide practical strategies to nurture this self-compassion and boost your self-esteem.

Strategies for Nurturing Self-Compassion and Boosting Self-Esteem

Self-compassion can feel like a foreign concept, primarily if you've grown accustomed to the chatter of your inner critic. However, with consistent practice, you can cultivate this vital skill and boost your self-esteem. Here are some strategies to help you nurture self-compassion:

1. **Mindful Awareness:** Notice your self-talk. Is it harsh? How you speak to yourself is the first step toward change. Like Sarah, judgmental, or kind and understanding? Becoming aware of how busy a healthcare professional, like herself, was frequently stressed and self-critical of themselves. After practicing mindfulness, she became aware of her more harsh inner dialogue and was able to start a kinder, compassionate tone.

2. **Positive Affirmations**: These are statements that can help you challenge and overcome self- sabotaging and negative thoughts. When you repeat them often and believe in them, you can start to make positive changes. From our earlier example,

Susan could affirm, "I'm doing my best, and that's good enough."

3. **Self-Care Rituals**: These don't have to be grand gestures. Even small acts like a 3-minute meditation with relaxing music, a short walk in the morning, having a cup of tea with your 'favorite' cup, decorating your room with beautiful flowers, taking a nice long bath with scented candles, or reading a book can work wonders in fostering a compassionate relationship with oneself. Look at Linda, a busy mother working two jobs. Despite her packed schedule, she dedicates 10 minutes each morning to quietly enjoying a cup of tea. This small act of kindness towards herself has dramatically increased her self-compassion.

4. **Professional Help:** If cultivating self-compassion feels overwhelming, seeking help from a coach or a therapist could provide the needed support. Like Jenny, a successful businesswoman who found therapy to be a powerful tool in turning her journey of self- compassion from an uphill battle into a fulfilling voyage of self-discovery and growth.

The path to self-compassion is not a straight one, and that's okay. It's a process, a journey. So, remember to extend patience and kindness to yourself as you walk this path. In the next section, we will explore how self-compassion can play a pivotal role in resilience and overcoming personal challenges.

As we conclude this chapter, let's take a moment to reflect on the transformational power of self-compassion. It's not about inflating our ego or wallowing in self-pity but acknowledging our imperfections with kindness, understanding, and patience. We've journeyed through the harsh terrain of self-criticism, discovered the healing power of self-kindness, and explored strategies to nurture self-compassion and boost self-esteem.

Remember Sarah, Susan, Linda, and Jenny? Their stories serve as a beacon, demonstrating that even amidst life's hustle and bustle, it's possible to cultivate a compassionate relationship with oneself. These women are no different from you; they, too, have their struggles, busy schedules, and dreams. The key lies in their commitment to prioritize self-compassion.

Embrace the concept of self-compassion and let it be your ally, not a luxury relegated to the backseat.

"I love myself for I am a beloved child of the universe, and the universe lovingly takes care of me now."

- Louise Hay

So, as we turn the page to the next chapter, carry this wisdom close to your heart: the journey to your dream life is paved with self-compassion, and it starts with being kind to the person in the mirror.

Chapter 3
Visioning Your Future Self - Living Your Dream Life

"Write it down 'The List of My Future' in your notebook, then imagine you are already there. Check your energy levels, feelings, thoughts, actions, and words. How close are you to your future self?"

- Rose Light

Welcome to Chapter 3: Having delved into the transformative journey of self-discovery and the nurturing power of self-compassion in the previous chapters, we are now poised to venture into the captivating world of personal growth and lifelong learning. In this chapter, we'll explore how continuous learning and embracing change can be catalysts for achieving your dream life. You'll meet inspiring characters who've harnessed the power of personal development to bring about profound changes in their lives. So, get comfortable and ready to uncover the intriguing links between personal growth, lifelong learning, and pursuing your dream life. It's time to spark your inner curiosity and embrace the journey of endless possibilities that personal growth promises!

Embracing the Power of Visualization and Setting Realistic, Personalized Goals

As we delve deeper into the path of living your dream life, let's focus on envisioning your future self. The power of visualization is like a hidden gem, often underestimated. This ability to project ourselves into the future, to see where we want to be and who we want to become, is a formidable tool in pursuing personal growth and fulfillment.

Imagine our protagonist, Zoe. She's a bustling executive at a leading tech firm. Her calendar is packed with meetings, her inbox overflowing with unread emails, and her mental bandwidth teetering at the edge. But even amidst this chaos, Zoe harbors a dream - she imagines herself living a life of calm, contributing to social good, and leading a tech non-profit that fosters education for underprivileged kids.

Zoe has a picture of this life in her mind. But to make it real, she realizes she needs more than a fuzzy mental image; she needs a solid, achievable plan. So, Zoe starts with setting realistic, personalized goals - not dictated by her boss, colleagues, or any societal expectations but derived from her own aspirations. She begins compartmentalizing her vision into tangible milestones, such as acquiring necessary skills, networking in the non-profit sector, and accumulating savings for a smoother transition. The magic of setting such goals is in the customization. For instance, Zoe's definition of 'necessary skills' might include leadership in a non-profit context, understanding fund allocation, and proficiency in social advocacy. These tailored to her vision, amplifying the chances of her success.

But there's another aspect to this journey that Zoe must pay attention to - embracing flexibility. Life doesn't always go as planned, and our visions of our future selves aren't immune to this truth. By factoring in the possibility of change and being open to modifying her goals, Zoe is able to equip herself to face unforeseen challenges.

Remember, visualizing our future self isn't just daydreaming about an ideal life. It's about breaking down that dream into practical steps, setting realistic and personalized goals, and preparing ourselves for a journey full of learnings, experiences, and occasional detours. And amidst all this, what remains crucial is the belief in our ability to shape our future - a belief that can turn even the most distant dreams into our living reality.

The Link Between Personal Growth, Lifelong Learning, and the Pursuit of a Dream Life

In the realm of personal growth, the equation is never a simple linear path. Instead, it's a spiraling, evolving, and interconnected process, where two of its key ingredients are lifelong learning and an unquenchable thirst to live one's dream life. When we mention lifelong learning, it's not just about returning to school or getting more degrees. It's a broader, more encompassing journey of growing and evolving. It involves a shift in mindset, seeing every experience, every interaction, and every challenge as an opportunity to learn and grow. It's about adopting a learner's mindset - being curious, open-minded, and persistent. The world becomes our classroom, each day a lesson, each moment a teacher.

Now, let's draw a connection to our dream life. Often, the vision we harbor for our dream life is an elevated version of our present self. And to ascend to this version, we must continuously learn, adapt, and evolve.

Meet Alex, a busy parent managing both a challenging career and a bustling household. She dreams of starting her own sustainable business, leaving a meaningful impact on the world while also achieving a healthier work-life balance. To reach this dream, Alex doesn't only need the basic knowledge of business operations. She needs to understand sustainability, learn the art of managing a flexible work schedule, adapt to the dynamism of entrepreneurship, and much more.

Alex dives headfirst into this vast ocean of knowledge. She listens to podcasts during her commute, takes online courses after tucking her kids into bed, and transforms her lunch breaks into mini-learning sessions. Through lifelong learning, Alex is inching closer to her dream life, and becoming a better version of herself each day.

In the grand scheme of things, our personal growth, our continuous learning, and the pursuit of our dream life are not separate threads but a beautifully woven tapestry of our existence. It's a cyclical process where our dream life fuels our desire to learn, and our learning brings us one step closer to our dream life.

In the next section, we will explore some real-life examples of individuals who, like Alex, have transformed their lives by maintaining a clear vision and steadfast determination. These narratives will illustrate how this process unfolds, providing you with tangible blueprints to inspire and guide your journey.

Case Studies of Women Who Transformed Their Lives Through a Clear Vision and Steadfast Determination

Let's dive into a couple of inspiring stories of real women who have transformed their lives by honing their visions and persisting relentlessly, demonstrating that dreams can, indeed, become a reality.

Case Study 1: Maya was in her mid-30s when she decided to turn her lifelong passion for photography into a full-time career. This was a challenging task, considering she had a full-time job. But her vision was clear - she envisioned a life where she could express her creativity daily while also making a living. She started by taking night classes on photography and business management. Gradually, she began offering free photoshoots to build a portfolio. Eventually, her determination paid off, and her unique vision allowed her to establish a successful photography business, showing her the power of following one's dreams.

Case Study 2: Lucy, a career-driven corporate lawyer, had always felt an inexplicable pull towards social work. However, the idea of leaving her high-paying job and starting afresh in her mid-40s seemed unrealistic. One day, she visualized her future self and realized she didn't want to look back on a life of regret. So she began working part-time for a non-profit while maintaining her law job. It was tough to juggle both, but Lucy was determined. Years later, she's now running her own non-profit and has never been happier.

Case Study 3: Jade was an accomplished accountant in her late 40s, but her heart longed for the culinary world. She daydreamed about owning a quaint bakery where she could bring joy to people with her mouth-watering pastries. The decision to leave a stable job and step into the unpredictable food industry was daunting, but Jade decided to visualize her future self. She began taking baking classes in the evening, tested her pastries at local farmer's markets, and saved diligently. Five years later, Jade's Bakery became the go-to place in her town, serving joy one pastry at a time. Her story is a testament to the power of a dream backed by a detailed vision and determination.

Case Study 4: Maria, a primary school teacher in her late 50s, had always had a penchant for adventure and travel. With her children grown up and her teaching career winding down, Maria saw an opportunity to pursue her passion for exploration. However, the thought of starting a new journey in her late 50s seemed daunting. But she had a clear vision of her future self as an intrepid traveler and blogger, inspiring older adults to follow their dreams. Maria started by taking small local trips and writing about her experiences. Her blog quickly gained traction, attracting readers with her humor, authenticity, and zest for life. Today, Maria has visited over 30 countries and inspired thousands of her readers to chase their dreams, irrespective of age.

These stories highlight that your age, your current obligations, or the length of your to-do list shouldn't inhibit you from striving toward your dream life. It may seem daunting initially, but by carving out a clear vision and backing it with unwavering determination, you too, can transform your life to live your dream life.

Remember that each person's path will be unique. There is no 'one size fits all' approach when it comes to building your dream life. It's about defining what happiness and success mean to you, so find what you really want in your dream life so that you can pour all your high energy and efforts much easier to get there; listen to your small voice and ask, "What do I really want to do even though people around me are not approving?" instead of listening to people's loud voices around you, and craft a path that fulfillment, a sense of purpose, and perhaps financial freedom, freedom from time, and associates by doing something you really enjoy. Keep your vision clear, your determination steadfast, and leads you there. It's all about personal growth, pushing your boundaries, and embracing lifelong learning. Your dream life is not some distant, unattainable concept. It's a mosaic of moments, experiences, and accomplishments that bring you joy, know that with each day, with each step, you are crafting your dream life.

In conclusion, Chapter 3 has taken us on a voyage into the future - the future of you. We've harnessed the power of visualization to set realistic, personalized goals, underlining the intimate links between personal growth, lifelong learning, and the pursuit of your dream life. Our journey was illuminated by the experiences of real-life women who, just like you, dared to envision a different future for themselves and achieved it through determination and a clear vision.

By embracing the transformative power of visualization and setting clear, achievable goals, we learn to move beyond the limitations of our current circumstances. Much like artists, we realize we can shape our destiny with intention and courage. And, in doing so, we become lifelong learners, open to new experiences and possibilities.

Life is a constant journey of self-discovery and growth. And the best part? There's no age limit, no expiration date on dreams. Whether you are in your 20s or your 60s, there is always time to envision your future self and create your dream life.

So as we turn the page to the next chapter, let's carry with us the inspiring stories of Maya, Lucy, Jade, and Maria. They remind us of what's possible when we dare to dream, plan, and relentlessly pursue our vision.

Chapter 4
Take Consistent Action

"Take more consistent action. It will lead you to an exciting future - Your Dream Life."

- Rose Light

Welcome to Chapter 4: Take Consistent Action. This is where the rubber meets the road. After embarking on the journey of self-discovery and defining our future vision in the previous chapters, it's time to set things into motion.

In this chapter, we will unravel the profound power of action and persistence in transforming your dreams into a reality. Objectives are crucial; they give us direction. But without action, they remain abstract and unattainable. Remember, it's not just about making big leaps but about taking small, consistent steps that build momentum over time, propelling you toward your goals.

We will also delve into some tried-and-true tools and techniques to keep your motivation high and help you overcome any hurdles that stand in your way. Consistency can sometimes be challenging, but it can become second nature with the right mindset and strategies.

This chapter will arm you with the practical know- how of how to create a blueprint for your actions and sustain the momentum needed to live your dream life. Buckle up and get ready to shift from dreaming to doing.

The Indispensable Role of Action and Persistence in Achieving Personal Goals

In this section of Chapter 4, we focus on the momentum of consistent action. As we continue our journey, it's critical to remember that dreaming is only the first part of the equation. The next, perhaps most crucial step, is to commit ourselves and start acting on those dreams persistently and passionately.

Imagine you are standing at the edge of a serene lake with a handful of pebbles. Each pebble represents a goal, a dream that you want to realize. Now, if you throw all the stones at once, you will create a big splash but few ripples. However, if you throw them one by one, each will create a unique pattern of ripples, reaching out far and wide across the lake. That's the power of consistent action, creating a cascade of effects that can reach beyond our initial efforts.

There's an old adage that goes, "The journey of a thousand miles begins with a single step." The essence of this quote perfectly encapsulates the concept of consistent action. Every step, no matter how small, contributes to realizing our dreams.

Here are a few steps you can incorporate into your life:

1. **Break It Down:** Big goals can feel overwhelming. Break them down into manageable parts. If you dream of writing a book, start with writing a paragraph daily.

2. **Create a Routine:** Consistency becomes more manageable when woven into our daily routine. Find a specific time each day to work towards your goal.

3. **Celebrate Small Wins:** Each step completed is a victory in itself. Don't wait until the end goal is reached. Celebrate every small win to keep the momentum going.

4. **Be Resilient:** There will be days when things don't go according to plan. Don't be disheartened. Learn from these experiences and keep moving forward.

5. **Seek Support:** Share your dreams and plans with someone you trust. They can provide support and encouragement.

Consistent action is like a snowball rolling down a hill - it starts small but gathers speed and size as it keeps moving. It's the steady, persistent actions that, over time, lead us to achieve our greatest dreams. Just like our case studies from Chapter 3, remember that it's not about making enormous changes all at once but about taking small, consistent steps toward your dream life. Your dream life is waiting, and it all starts with that first step. Take it today, take it tomorrow, and keep stepping forward. Let's build momentum together. It's time to turn your dreams into a reality, one

Tools and Techniques for Staying Motivated and Surmounting Obstacles

A major part of consistent action involves maintaining motivation and overcoming obstacles that come our way. Staying motivated when life gets busy or when challenges arise is a struggle many face. This path is seldom smooth in pursuing our dream life, but every speed bump can be conquered with the right tools and techniques.

One effective way of sustaining motivation is by visualizing your end goal. It's not just about seeing the big picture but envisioning how you'll feel once you've achieved it. This emotional connection with your plan can provide a mighty push,especially during trying times. Regularly remind yourself of why you started and how every step, no matter how small, brings you closer to your dream life.

Breaking your big goal into smaller, manageable tasks is another valuable strategy. Accomplishing these tasks can provide a sense of progress and achievement, fueling your motivation further. Remember, it's not about overnight transformation but continuous, steady improvement. When faced with a daunting task, break it down. Instead of focusing on writing a book, focus on writing a page. You'll soon realize that the sum of these small tasks leads to considerable progress.

Another tool in your arsenal should be a supportive community, be it friends, family, or like - minded individuals pursuing similar goals. Share your journey, victories, and challenges. The power of collective energy and mutual support can't be understated.

Additionally, embrace a growth mindset, viewing challenges and failures as learning opportunities rather than roadblocks. When you stumble, don't wallow in self-pity. Instead, ask yourself, "What can I learn from this?" and "How can I use this to grow?" This mindset will enable you to transform obstacles into stepping stones toward your dream life.

Finally, self-care is vital in this journey. Physical health and mental well-being play an essential role in maintaining your drive. Eat healthily, exercise regularly, get enough rest, and make time for activities that rejuvenate you. A healthy body and mind contribute to a sustained motivation level, enabling you to face challenges head-on.

These tools and techniques are not a one-size-fits-all solution. They need to be customized according to your personal preferences and life circumstances. The key lies in adopting a set of strategies that work for you and applying them consistently. Remember, the journey to living your dream life is not a sprint but a marathon. Consistency is your faithful companion in this journey. Keep moving, one step at a time, and before you know it, you'll be living the life you've always envisioned.

Inspiring Examples of the Remarkable Outcomes Driven by Consistent Action

The magic of consistent action isn't just a concept; it's an observable reality in many who dared to dream and persist. Let's explore a few inspiring examples of remarkable outcomes driven by consistent action.

Consider Ellie, a full-time nurse. For years, she dreamt of becoming an author. Despite her demanding schedule, she committed to writing for just 15 minutes daily. It was a challenge at first, trying to fit this new routine amidst a whirlwind of responsibilities. But Ellie was tenacious. Little by little, those precious minutes accumulated, and after a year, she had the first draft of her novel.

Then there's Tony, a high-school teacher with a passion for painting. His job was fulfilling but left little time for his artistic pursuits. Determined not to let his passion fade, Tony started waking up an hour earlier each morning to paint. His consistency not only helped him improve his skills, but he also eventually held his first solo art exhibit.

Another powerful example is Mary, a successful lawyer who had always been fascinated by coding. Despite her limited time, she enrolled in an online course, dedicating a few hours each week to learn this new skill. It was a slow process, but she didn't lose her heart. A couple of years later, Mary transitioned into a rewarding career in tech, blending her legal expertise with her new coding skills.

Finally, let's talk about Samantha, who decided to get fit in her 40s. The gym was a foreign world to her, and the workouts seemed grueling. Instead of giving up, Samantha decided to take small, consistent steps. She started with just 10 minutes of exercise daily, gradually increasing her workout duration and intensity. A year later, not only did she achieve her fitness goals, but she also completed her first marathon.

These stories exemplify the power of consistent action. Each of these individuals had full lives, busy schedules, and ample reasons to put off their personal dreams. Yet, they chose to act, persist, and make remarkable strides toward their personal goals. These aren't overnight success stories but the fruits of consistent action and determination. Remember, it's not about grand gestures but about showing up for your dreams, one day at a time. As you embark on this journey towards your dream life, let their stories be your beacon, reminding you that every step counts, no matter how small.

And so, we conclude this exploration of the critical role of consistent action in crafting our dream life. Through this chapter, we've understood the power of perseverance, been introduced to various tools and techniques to stay motivated, and looked at real-life examples that testify to the magic of consistency.

Remember, while dreaming and envisioning are essential, it is your actions that truly shape your life.

Consistent action, no matter how small, is the bridge that connects your present to your envisioned future. It is the engine that propels you forward, helps you overcome obstacles, and brings you closer to your personal goals each day.

Let us keep in mind that consistency isn't about perfection or immediacy. It's about showing up for yourself, day after day, even when things are tough. The path to our dream life isn't a sprint; it's more of a marathon, where resilience and consistency trump speed.

Associate with positive people who are content with your happiness. They can provide support and encouragement but don't associate with negative people who disapprove of your joy. Don't keep or bring them into your inner circle. Don't waste your time worrying what they might think about you or your plan, and don't let them impede you and your future - your dream life, when you move your mindset from "someday in the future" to "now," your life will start moving towards your dream.

Believe in yourself, regardless of the circumstances, even when you struggle to believe, enjoy each process, and move forward. When you deal with challenges, don't wait until you think you're well prepared and ready; take the initiative to take the first step, and even if you begin moving backward, focus again on what makes you happy, and take the time to appreciate those things fully. By believing in yourself, you have the power to figure out what makes you happy and to fulfill your dreams. As long as you do your best to act and pour out your energy toward your goals, your life won't be the same. So relax, and enjoy the process. And don't forget to place your "favorite" items around you to lift your spirit, such as flowers, crystals, sentimental items, and so on.

In the coming chapters, we will delve deeper into other critical elements of living your dream life. For now, reflect on the power of consistent action and think about the first small step you will take. After all, as Lao Tzu wisely stated, "The journey of a thousand miles begins with a single step." Remember, every step counts and every day is a new opportunity to move closer to your dream life.

Chapter 5

Be Likable and Receive Support

"Surround yourself only with positive people who will lift your energy levels and expect positive outcomes."

- Rose Light

In Chapter 5, "Be Likable and Receive Support," we will explore the pivotal role our relationships and support systems play in the quest for our dream life. As human beings, we are fundamentally social creatures. Our connections to others, the bridges we build and maintain, significantly impact our life trajectories. These relationships can motivate us, provide us with a sounding board, and, most importantly, offer us much needed support during times of struggle.

However, creating and nurturing the right relationships is an art in itself. It's about surrounding ourselves with positivity, finding those who push us towards growth and acceptance, and learning how to lean on others without losing our sense of self. It is about building a network that not only supports us but also challenges us to be better and do better.

In this chapter, we'll dive into the science of social connections and explore practical advice and strategies for nurturing beneficial relationships. We'll also look at how to draw boundaries when needed and how to cultivate a support system that respects your aspirations and values.

By the end of the chapter: you'll have the knowledge and cultivate a network of relationships that propel you forward toward your dream life.

The Significance of Cultivating Positive Relationships and Nurturing a Supportive Network in Personal Development

In our quest to live our dream life, we often overlook one crucial aspect - the relationships we cultivate along the way. Relationships are like bridges that connect us to our aspirations, dreams, and successes. They offer emotional support, share in our joys and sorrows, motivate us when we falter, and provide a fresh perspective when we feel stuck.

Picture your dream life for a moment. Imagine achieving that dream without the support, encouragement, and love from those around you. A bit bleak, isn't it? That's because the journey toward our dream life isn't a solo expedition. It's a voyage that thrives on the interplay of relationships and mutual support.

Consider this - every successful person, from visionaries like Elon Musk to changemakers like Nelson Mandela, can attribute a part of their success to the support of the people around them. Relationships act as a robust support system, a sort of cheerleading squad, helping us remain resilient and focused on our journey.

However, building bridges isn't just about connecting with others. It's about building healthy, fulfilling, positive connections aligning with our values and aspirations. Healthy relationships can significantly enhance our quality of life, bringing joy, companionship, and a sense of belonging. On the other hand, toxic or draining relationships can act as hurdles in our path, leading to stress, self-doubt, and hindered progress.

Moreover, relationships play a significant role in our personal development. Engaging with diverse individuals broadens our perspectives, helps us understand different viewpoints, and fosters empathy and compassion. It encourages us to step out of our comfort zone and grow as individuals, which is critical in our journey toward our dream life.

So, let's get to the heart of the matter - how do we cultivate positive relationships and build a supportive network? As we move forward in this chapter, we'll delve into some practical tips and strategies to foster and maintain relationships that act as stepping stones toward your dream life.

Remember, relationships are a two-way street that requires effort, understanding, and patience. And every bridge you build is an investment that brings you one step closer to your dream life. So, let's start building these bridges together!

Practical Tips for Fostering and Maintaining Healthy Relationships

Building and maintaining healthy relationships may seem daunting, especially in today's fast-paced world, but it's not impossible. Here are some practical tips to help foster these all-important connections:

1. **Be Proactive**: Don't wait for others to make the first move. Reach out, introduce yourself, ask about their day, or initiate a conversation about a common interest. It's about taking small steps toward building a connection. If you realize that it's okay to be yourself, you can relax and know that you don't need to compare yourself with others, which can reduce your stress.

2. **Communication is Key**: Honest and open communication forms the bedrock of any healthy relationship. Express your feelings, be it joy, concern, or even disappointment, with tact and understanding. It not only fosters trust but also encourages the other person to do the same. If you are a leader, trust people and delegate tasks instead of measuring them with high expectations. And instead of looking for people's faults, focus on their good qualities. Appreciate people more than what they did, even if it wasn't anything special; the world can be a precious treasure that people want to keep deep inside their hearts forever or a sharp sword that leaves pain in their hearts for the rest of their lives. So, be extremely careful when you choose the words. Try using words that encourage and motivate people.

These are the words that I want to tell myself.

It's okay to be myself.

My "Job" is a tool to enjoy my life.

What do I really want to do?

Don't worry about how some people might react to words because it's more important to communicate with those who like you and will follow you. It's normal to feel uncomfortable around some people, and there's nothing wrong with not wanting to associate with them. You have the choice to associate with positive people who actually like you.

1. **Active Listening:** While expressing ourselves is essential, equally crucial is lending an attentive ear to what others have to say. Active listening entails not merely hearing but understanding, empathizing, and responding constructively.

2. **Respect Boundaries:** Every relationship thrives on a balance of personal space and closeness. Understand and respect the other person's boundaries. This balance can differ from person to person, and it's important to adjust and respect those differences.

3. **Be There:** Support isn't just about being there in times of distress; it's about celebrating the joys too. Share in their happiness, support them in their ventures and lend a shoulder when they need to lean.

4. **Be Yourself:** Authenticity goes a long way in forming solid and fulfilling relationships. Embrace your quirks, your strengths, and your vulnerabilities. Real connections happen when people interact with the 'real' you.

5. **Mutual Growth:** Healthy relationships involve growing together. Celebrate each other's achievements, motivate one another, and learn from each other. Be each other's cheerleader on the journey of personal growth.

6. **Patience and Forgiveness:** Remember, no one's perfect, and mistakes happen. Patience and forgiveness go a long way in healing and strengthening relationships.

These tips are like building blocks for fostering and maintaining healthy relationships. However, remember, the process is iterative, and it's okay if everything doesn't fall into place right away. The goal is to make progress, however small, each day toward building bridges that support and enrich our lives.

In the next section, we'll dive into some stories of women whose lives have been significantly enriched through strong social connections and support.

Their stories are a testament to the power of positive relationships in our journey toward living the dream life. So stay tuned!

Stories of Women Whose Lives Were Enriched Through Strong Social Connections and Support

Let's dive into the lives of two women who brilliantly illustrate the importance of building bridges through relationships and support.

First, meet Ada, a full-time corporate executive. Despite her relentless schedule, Ada found herself feeling isolated and overwhelmed. She decided to reach out and build a support network, starting with her colleagues. She proactively initiated conversations, participated in team-building activities, and showed a genuine interest in others' lives. Ada also began attending local community events, where she made connections with individuals who had similar interests and challenges. Over time, she built a network of support that helped her navigate her busy life and feel less isolated. The sense of belonging and shared experiences boosted her mental health, ultimately making her more resilient and capable in all aspects of her life.

Then there's Beth, a young entrepreneur who realized the power of positive relationships when she launched her start-up. She found her first few clients through her network, got recommendations for trustworthy vendors, and even met her business partner. She made it a point to maintain these relationships, often through quick check-ins or lunch meetings. By fostering these connections, Beth didn't just grow her business but found mentors, friends, and a community of fellow entrepreneurs. Her story is a testament to the fact that the bridges we build can take us places we never imagined.

These stories illustrate that no matter where you are in life or what our dreams may be, building and maintaining strong relationships is a crucial part of your journey. It's like building a bridge. It may seem daunting at first, but once you've laid down the foundational bricks, it becomes a path that connects you to others, provides support when needed, and ultimately leads you to your dream life.

Remember, it's about living your dream life, so knowing who you associate with and the relationships you foster along the way is essential. These connections will become part of your life's wealth, enriching your journey as you live your dream life. Building bridges is, therefore, not a solitary act but a community endeavor that adds value to both your life and the lives of those who you connect with.

In conclusion, this chapter highlights the critical role that relationships and support networks play in our lives. As we strive to live our dream lives, we must understand that we are not solitary islands. We are social beings, interconnected with others in myriad ways. Building bridges with those around us provides us not only with emotional and practical support but also enriches our journey. Whether through shared experiences, valuable advice, or a shoulder to lean on in tough times, these connections add layers of richness to our lives. The stories of Ada and Beth exemplify the transformative power of relationships and underscore the importance of fostering and maintaining them, irrespective of our busy schedules. Form positive relationships with the people we meet, be likable, and receive support.

Chapter 6

Chance, Luck, and Coincidence Bring Your Miracles

"Count your blessings, and be grateful for all the good things that are in your life. Your positive energy makes you happy and creates a better environment for you."

- Rose Light

In life, some of our most impactful moments come not from meticulous planning but from the unexpected and serendipitous. Welcome to Chapter 6, 'Chance, Luck, Coincidence Bring Your Miracles.' In this chapter, we delve into the transformative power of these random encounters and unforeseen opportunities.

It's about recognizing chance, luck, and coincidence and letting them bring your miracles as well as having a mindset that involves openness, adaptability, and resilience. It's about embracing the unexpected twists and turns that life offers. We'll share stories of individuals who have harnessed this power, turning chance events into meaningful shifts in their life paths.

May this chapter help you understand chance, luck, and coincidence and that sometimes, the route to your dream life can be a confusing, unexpected journey that is as beautiful as the destination - your dream life.

Understanding the Role of Chance, Luck, Coincidence in Life, and the Importance of Being Prepared to Seize Opportunities

Chance, luck, and coincidence - those delightful moments when the unexpected happens, and it catapults our life into a new, exciting direction.

It feels like magic, doesn't it? As if the stars aligned, and fate reached out its hand to guide us. Is it all about cosmic luck, or is something more at play?

In our busy, structured lives, it's easy to overlook serendipity's role. We plan our careers, our goals, and our days down to the minute, but we can only plot out some things. Some of the most transformative experiences often come from t h e unplanned and chance encounters, and the opportunities we didn't even know existed until

Understanding and acknowledging the role of chance, luck, and coincidence in our lives doesn't mean we abandon our plans or goals. On the contrary, it means we open ourselves to the possibility of other routes to achieving those goals, some that we might not have considered. It's about broadening our perspective to recognize and seize opportunities, whether they align with our initial plans or not.

Think of chance, luck, and coincidence as a friendly ally, a co-conspirator in your journey towards your dream life. It's like setting off on a road trip with a destination in mind but being willing to take an unexpected opportunity when you see an interesting sign. Sometimes, that opportunity leads to an unforgettable adventure that highlights your journey.

So how do we ready ourselves for these moments of opportunity? It starts with cultivating an open mindset that is curious, flexible, and receptive to change. It's about not just looking straight ahead but expanding our field of vision to spot the opportunities at the periphery.

There are numerous examples of people who have harnessed the power of chance, luck, and coincidence to reach their goals:

These individuals recognized chance, luck, and coincidence. They were active participants, tuned in to their own environment, open to new experiences, and prepared to seize opportunities as they arose. As we delve deeper into this chapter, remember that unexpected opportunity isn't just a whimsical concept. It's a powerful force, and with the right mindset, it can become a crucial component of living your dream life.

Understanding Chance, Luck, and Coincidence and the Law of Attraction: How Chance, Luck, and Coincidence Bring Your Miracles

The law of attraction draws opportunities and experiences to ourselves through our thoughts and intentions. It's about aligning our energies and actions with our goals. It implies that we have an active role in what happens to us. When you recognize that chance, luck, and coincidence, bring your miracles, be ready to seize those opportunities and have the courage and openness to grab hold of them.

Here's how You Can Tip the Scales in Your Favor:

- **Develop a Broad Network**: The more diverse your connections, the higher your chances of encountering unexpected opportunities.

- **Step Out of Your Comfort Zone**: Engage in new experiences. Join that business event, start that blog, and reach out to someone you admire.

- **Stay Curious and Observant**: Keep your mind open, ask questions, and be aware of your surroundings.

- **Embrace Flexibility**: Be willing to pivot and adapt when things don't go according to your plan. Sometimes, the change is in the path.

- **Nurture a Positive Mindset**: Believe in yourself, the possibility of good things happening, and that you can spot them when they do.

The key is not to wait but to cultivate an environment where the opportunity is more likely to occur. The world is brimming with opportunities, but we often miss them because we must prepare and be open to them. Cultivate the mindset, and you'll be amazed at how the universe conspires to help you live your dream life.

Diverse Examples of Women Who Turned Chance Encounters and Events into Major Life-Altering Moments

Countless women have recognized chance, luck, and coincidence as a powerful catalysts in their lives. One such example is Arlene, a corporate lawyer. Arlene worked long hours, often too exhausted to pursue her passion for writing. One day, while typing away on her work laptop at a cafe, a sudden downpour forced her to share her table with a stranger. That stranger happened to be a literary agent who noticed her screen filled with both legal documents and short stories. A casual conversation turned into a fruitful relationship, and Arlene finally started her journey as a published author. A chance encounter that day turned into a major life-altering moment.

Then there was Kelly, a woman who juggled two jobs while dreaming of owning a bakery. A random conversation with a stranger at the grocery checkout line about her love for banking led to a surprising investment opportunity. The stranger, a local businessman, was looking for a unique venture. He was so impressed with Kelly's passion and delicious homemade samples that he backed her dream. A fortuitous encounter turned into a dream come true for Kelly.

And who can forget Jane, a dedicated nurse? During a particularly challenging shift at the hospital, Jane helped a woman cope with her husband's surgery. The woman turned out to be a well-connected philanthropist who was so touched by Jane's compassion that she helped her set up a community outreach program for medical awareness - something Jane had envisioned for years.

These women didn't just wait for their dreams to become reality; they knew chance, luck, and coincidence to bring their miracles. They remained open to opportunities, talked about their passions, and, most importantly, were prepared when the chance came knocking.

Such stories serve as powerful reminders that life's landscape is dotted with hidden treasures waiting to be discovered. The world unfolds to those open and prepared to receive its gifts. Write down the "list of your future" in your "favorite" notebook. Discover yourself and prepare yourself by counting your blessings, and being grateful for all the good things in your life. Your positive energy makes you happy and creates a better environment for you. It's not about meticulous planning but recognizing the power of unexpected opportunities from the universe, and seeing where it takes you to your dream life.

And so, as we close this chapter, remember to: listen to your small voice, choose the right things that make you happy, figure out what's your direction, understand that it's okay to make mistakes and that it's better to try than to do nothing at all, consistently believe in yourself and prepare yourself to not worry and to relax, and that unexpected opportunities bring your miracles. Let life surprise you as you journey towards your dream life.

Chapter 7

Power of Thoughts - Your Emotions, Actions, and Your Life

"You can overcome challenges by changing your thoughts and emotions and finding the courage and energy to take action."

-   Rose Light

Welcome to Chapter 7, where we embark on the most profound journey of all: into the beautiful labyrinth of our minds. This is a realm where thoughts bloom like wildflowers and emotions flow like mighty rivers, each shaping the contours of our lives. Here, we'll learn to navigate these intricate pathways, harnessing our power to cultivate a flourishing garden of dreams. Let's master the symphony of thoughts and emotions, creating a melody that propels us toward our dream life.

Exploring the Influence of Thoughts and Emotions on Actions and Overall Life Outcomes

Imagine your thoughts and emotions as a powerful engine that drives your actions and shapes your world. These mental processes, whether we are consciously aware of them or not, significantly affect our decisions, behaviors, and overall life outcomes. They can be our greatest allies in pursuing our dream life or our most challenging foes, depending on how we manage them.

Thoughts and emotions are inherently linked; they feed off each other in an endless loop. Your thoughts can trigger a cascade of emotions, which in turn can influence your subsequent thoughts and actions. For instance, imagine you're in a bustling cafe, trying to finish a report before a deadline. A thought like "I'll never finish this on time" can trigger feelings of stress and anxiety, which could lead to procrastination or lack of focus, thus making the initial thought a self-fulfilling prophecy.

Just as a negative thought can have a domino effect, positive thoughts can do the same, but in a beneficial way. Think of that same situation, but this time, the thought is, "I can do this. I've faced tighter deadlines before." Suddenly, a surge of confidence and determination takes hold, powering you through the task and bringing the thought to fruition.

Understanding this dynamic underscores why gaining control over your thoughts and emotions is vital to living your dream life. You might not have control over external events, but you have a say in how you interpret and react to them. It's not the events that shape your life but your responses to them. It's important to clarify that this doesn't mean suppressing or ignoring negative thoughts and emotions. These are a natural part of the human experience and can serve as valuable signals or catalysts for change. The goal here isn't to cultivate a Pollyanna-like denial of life's challenges but to foster resilience and a positive outlook to help you navigate them more effectively.

In the next section, we'll delve into practical techniques for managing negative thoughts and emotions, fostering a positive mindset, and thus paving the way for a life that aligns with your dreams and aspirations. Remember, your mind is like a garden, and your thoughts are like seeds - it's time to grow a beautiful bouquet of life outcomes.

Techniques for Managing Negative Thoughts and Emotions and Fostering a Positive Mindset

Taming the tempests of the mind and soothing the seas of the heart are no easy feats. But learning to dance with our thoughts and emotions, rather than against them, can be incredibly liberating and a crucial step toward living your dream life. Here are some techniques to manage negative thoughts and emotions and cultivate a thriving mindset.

1. **Mindfulness**: Embrace your thoughts and emotions as they come, without judgment. By observing your inner experiences, you become better at discerning between constructive and destructive thoughts, giving you the power to decide which ones should hold sway.

2. **Reframing:** Transform negative thinking by changing the narrative. Instead of seeing a challenge as a hurdle, view it as an opportunity for growth. It's about recognizing the silver linings and becoming the author of your own story.

3. **Gratitude practice:** Maintaining a gratitude notebook or simply acknowledging the good in your day can shift your focus from what's going wrong to what's going right, fostering positivity.

4. **Meditation:** Meditation calms the mind, helps in stress reduction, and fosters emotional health. You don't need a secluded mountain or hours of free time - just a few minutes daily can make a big difference.

5. **Physical activity**: Regular exercise isn't just good for your body but also good for your mind. It releases endorphins, the body's natural mood boosters.

6. **Affirmations:** Create and use affirmations that resonate with your dreams and values. These positive statements, when repeated consistently, can change your thought patterns.

Remember, every person's journey to emotional and cognitive mastery is unique. What works for one may not work for another. It's about exploration and discovery. Some days may be more challenging than others, but each step you take is a step closer to mastering your mind and, in turn, moving closer to your dream life.

In the following section, we'll share some real-life accounts of women who've turned the tide, transforming their lives by mastering their thoughts and emotions. These stories prove that with a resolute mind and spirited heart, we can script our destiny, one thought, one emotion at a time.

Real-Life Accounts of Women Who Transformed Their Lives Through Cognitive and Emotional Mastery

Consider Sarah, a single woman working two jobs and barely making ends meet. She was frequently caught in a whirlpool of negative thoughts, often asking herself, "Why me?" One day, her friend handed her a gratitude jar she'd made at work, explaining how jotting down good things could make her happier. Deciding to try it, Sarah noted things she was thankful for, even if it was just a warm cup of tea on a cold morning. Gradually, she noticed a shift in her perception. Life still had its ups and downs, but the gratitude jar helped her focus on the positives, boosting her resilience.

Then there's Monica, a high-flying executive plagued with work stress and mounting health issues. A friend suggested she try meditation. Skeptical but desperate, Monica took a leap of faith. She started with just 3 minutes a day. Surprisingly, Monica began to find a sense of calm and clarity she hadn't felt in years. She could better manage her stress, and her decision-making improved. This small step profoundly changed her life, career, and health.

Lastly, meet Lily, an aspiring writer facing a string of rejections. Doubt began to cloud her mind, and she toyed with the idea of giving up. One day, she stumbled upon the concept of affirmations.

Intrigued, she decided to pen down an affirmation for herself, "I am a successful and talented writer. My words touch people's hearts." Initially, it felt strange and unreal, but her self-doubt subsided as days turned into weeks. She started writing, this time with a renewed vigor and confidence. Eventually, she bagged a publishing deal, her perseverance and self-belief finally paid off.

These stories remind us of the transformative power that lies within our minds. We can become the masters of our thoughts and emotions by guiding them towards step today because the most significant journey begins with a single step

"Master your mind, and you'll hold the key to shaping your reality. Let your thoughts be the architect of your dream life."

Future Meeting Note: *To find the right fit and live your dream life, you must first understand yourself. What do you like? What do you want to do? What is your dream? Let's write it down and find your best future life.*

- How do you want to feel every single day?

- What would make you happy?

- What would you do to make yourself happy today?

- What do you want to accomplish today?

- If you could make your wishes come true, what do you desire?

- What can you do today to make your wishes come true?

- How would you feel if you could have what you desire?

- Who do you want to appreciate today?

- Who do you want to make happy today?

- What kind of person do you want to be?

- Look at all questions and your answers, and then write down everything you like.

- Look at all questions and your answers, and then write down everything you want to do.

- What do you not like and not want to do? And how would you feel if they disappeared from your life?

- Let's write it down your top ten wishes.

Conclusion

You are a Masterpiece, and Your Dream Life is There for You

Remember that the power lies within you for the journey towards living your dream life. Every thought you think, every emotion you feel, paints the canvas of your life. Embrace positivity, bask in mindfulness, and seek happiness in the ordinary. The everyday miracles, the simple pleasures, truly make life extraordinary. Please don't give up; it leads to a place of wonder, fulfillment, and joy. Your dream life is there for you, and the journey starts and ends with you.

In the grand scheme of living your dream life, each step we've journeyed through plays a crucial role. It begins with the Power of Self-Awareness, understanding the beauty of your unique self, embracing the potential within, and setting a compass for your life's journey.

We then set Powerful Goals, tangible targets that guide us toward our dream life. With goals in place, we delve into the Power of Action, embracing the spirit of perseverance, determination, and courage. Every step, every move you make, counts - no action is too small in pursuing your dreams.

Be Likable and Receive Support, chapter 5, reminds us of the importance of connections, relationships, and support networks. The bonds we form nourish our emotional well-being and open doors to opportunities that bring us closer to our dreams.

In chapter 6, Chance, Luck, and Coincidence Bring Your Miracles, we learned that luck is chance and how essential being open, ready, and willing to seize life's opportunities are. Fortune, after all, favors the prepared.

The Power of Thoughts taught us about the power of thoughts and emotions. Through controlling our thoughts and managing our emotions, we find the strength to overcome obstacles and cultivate a mindset conductive to success.

In conclusion, the journey toward living your dream life intertwines with pursuing happiness, positivity, and mindfulness. It is a path filled with self-discovery, personal growth, and relentless pursuit of joy. Embrace the journey, cherish the lessons, and above all, remember - your dream life is there for you, and the journey starts and ends within you.

Remember, you hold the pen that writes the narrative of your life. Each moment presents an opportunity to author a new page, chapter, or even a new volume of your life's story. Embrace the challenges, celebrate the victories, and learn from the setbacks. They are just stepping stones on your path to living the dream life you've envisioned.

Remember, you are powerful beyond measure, and your potential is limitless. Your dream life is there for you. Take control, be proactive, and remember, every sunrise gives birth to a new day filled with opportunities to move closer to your dreams.

It's not about changing from an "ordinary person" to an "exceptional person" but discovering that "you are a masterpiece" and returning to the "original: who you are." You can be born with something other than an exceptional talent or be a chosen person. You only need to be a person who counts blessings, appreciates the good things in life, and enjoys living a dream life.

When you truly understand yourself and enjoy living "your" life, you will live your desired dream life.

Your dream life - A life where you can fully embrace who you are, what you do, and how you impact the world around you. It's a life filled with joy, love, fulfillment, and endless possibility.

You are the author of your life, the master of your mind, and the architect of your dreams. This is your story. Your journey. Your dream life.

When you enjoy your life, you will shine like a star. Then your life will encourage others to act and count their blessings.

It's your turn to shine. Are you ready? Enjoy your life, and it will take you to your dream life. You are a masterpiece!

Congratulations! Note from Author

Thank you for reading my book. I hope you enjoyed it. I'd be grateful if this book inspired you to build your desired life and journey towards living your dream life. I'd like to hear what chapter you enjoyed most and what ideas you have put into practice. When you have a moment, **would you mind taking 30 seconds to leave a quick review for this book?**

Having a positive review from you will help this book reach many more people like yourself so that they can benefit from the information shared within this book as well.

These reviews will help Authors produce more books like this that will help you get the results you want. So, if you enjoyed it, please let me know! :)

Lastly, don't forget to download your **gift, "5 Steps To Developing an Abundance Mindset."**

Just go to: **https://hello-rose-light.systeme.io/ free-gift-f447d39b**

To **connect with Rose Light**, visit at:

facebook.com/Rose-Light
instagram.com/rose.pearl.crystal
twitter.com/rose_light8

You are a masterpiece.

Believe in yourself. Trust your life.

Your dream life is there for you.

With Love,

Rose Light